Blackbird Singing at Dusk

Blackbird Singing at Dusk

Wendy Pratt

Nine
Arches
Press

Blackbird Singing at Dusk
Wendy Pratt

ISBN: 978-1-916760-02-8
eISBN: 978-1-916760-03-5

Copyright © Wendy Pratt, 2024.

Cover artwork: 'Hidden in the Crab Apples' © Gary & Heather Ramskill. www.littleramstudio.etsy.com

All rights reserved. No part of this work may be reproduced, stored or transmitted in any form or by any means, graphic, electronic, recorded or mechanical, without the prior written permission of the publisher.

Wendy Pratt has asserted their right under Section 77 of the Copyright, Designs and Patents Act 1988 to be identified as the author of this work.

First published November 2024 by:

Nine Arches Press
Unit 14, Sir Frank Whittle Business Centre,
Great Central Way, Rugby.
CV21 3XH
United Kingdom

www.ninearchespress.com

Printed in the United Kingdom on recycled paper by Imprint Digital.

Nine Arches Press is supported using public funding by Arts Council England.

For Matilda, always

Contents

When I bring you my body and tell you it is the landscape I grew up in	11
The Men Who Drive Tractors	12
The Boulder's Dream	13
After Chapel the Women Return	14
Self-Portrait as Bronze Age Burial Mound	15
Study of My Great, Great Grandfather Outside the Family Farm	16
Boulder Song	17
Self-Portrait Existing as a Fat Woman	18
Quern Stone, Sewerby, Grave 41	19
Sometimes I Pretend I am a Dog	20
Twelve Hour Working Day as a Golden Shovel	22
The Internalisation of Imposter Syndrome by the Rural Working Class Writer	23
My Dad on the Dark Side of the Moon	24
Concealment of Birth, 1846	26
Excavating the Bone House	27
The Tea Towel Game	34
the day I hit a blackbird	35
Jackdaws	36
Metal Detecting	37
Blackbird Singing at Dusk	38
Drone	39
Ground Nesting Bees	40
Slow Summer Poem of the Morning	41
Miracle of the Solstice	42
Thirteen ways of listening to a blackbird	43
Miracle of the Peas	46
Dales Engineering	48
Sara Lee	49
A Guide to Metal Detecting	50
Eleven	51

The Cat Brings Me a Live Sparrow, April 2020	53
Body of the Shrew	54
Talking to My Father as We Drive to the Second Chemo Appointment	55
Woe Water Fails to Rise	56
19th Century Cowbell	57
The water in my village	58
Thoughts on Deer Grazing at the Cemetery on the Day My Daughter Would Have Been Twelve Years Old	59
Intensive Care Unit Two	60
Thirteen	61
Boulder Returning in Echoes of Self	62
Acknowledgements and Thanks	65

When I bring you my body and tell you it is the landscape I grew up in

I am talking about the oilseed rape
that lay a thick layer of yellow
on my school uniform.

When I tell you how my body
moves in the wild, I am talking about
the semi-detached house my ex-farming family owned,
the aspirations to have something other
than soil beneath their fingernails.

> My body in this context is not earth
> and rocks and sky and moor, but blood
> and bone, the isotopes that sit in the teeth
> of my ancestors, the genes that crick my face
> to the shape of theirs.

When I bring you my body and ask you
to touch me, I'm talking about
the sea on all sides of me
and my body a shoreline.

> My body in this context is not sand
> but the carapaces of tiny creatures
> crushed into sand, the cartilage-star
> of a thornback ray, a lone albatross.

When I bring you my body
and tell you it is the landscape I grew up in,
I mean for you to look at me, hovering above me
as a hunting kestrel would: my stretch-mark/crop-marks
the ghosts of my settlements, burial mounds, stone tools,
jet beads and the fingerprint; the maker's mark pressed hard
into the pot sherds of my hip bones.

The Men Who Drive Tractors

Some of the men drive tractors
too fast down the lane
as if they are riding a great red bull

into a Greek myth and my existence
is as background to their story.
I have lived in many places

and this is often how the story is told:
I am so often the tree or the fence
and so rarely the bird singing at dusk,

stopping the world.

The Boulder's Dream

now it's to be moved and given its story back
  not just a boulder
in the form of an iron plaque
but a Shap granite   erratic boulder

not just a boulder
    they've moved it to widen the road
Shap granite   an erratic boulder
    they're moving everything to widen our world

    they've moved it to widen the road
to build a bridge   over the train track   a bypass
they're moving everything to widen our world
a supermarket where the cattle market was

    they're building a bridge over the train track   a bypass
I am watching the crane's sling going taut   then slack
    there's a supermarket where the cattle market was
    now it's to be moved and given its story back

After Chapel the Women Return

They are leaving the scriptures of men,
the comfort of psalms and hymns
and spreading out across the village:
a squadron of women in formation,
a flock homing in on slippers
and aprons, being called back by the hiss
of pressure cookers, the hum of Radio 4.

There is some wicked magic
in the way they peel potato skins; the paring knife
loose in the palm, the string-bound handle
gripped in the crease, just so. This is the way that women
have always held knives, even when knives were stones.

The women offer up their heritage
to anyone who will acknowledge it, eat of it.

They are massing in their kitchens,
the smoke of hot lard rising from pudding tins.
My mother is checking her own mother's cookbook
for meat timings, the scribble in the margins,
bringing her back in a way that prayers cannot.

Self-Portrait as Bronze Age Burial Mound

The hearth is my heart. I am
rooms of darkness and forgotten light.
My language is the mid-winter sun.

Whale-backed. Face-down.
Burrowed into by rabbits.
Burrowed into by rats.
Ashes and teeth are my language.

I carry the weight of responsibility.
I am detailed in archaeological sketches,
I appear huge on old maps, I loom
on the skyline.

My thoughts and secrets are in museums.
A sign says *Do Not Touch*.

Sometimes I am magical.
I face the east and promise
a kind of reinvention.

I am a receptacle for imagination, men
dig into me searching for riches.
I remain and remain and remain.

My language is the thumbnail mark
on the rim of a pot sherd, a carefully placed
lintel and doorway for a door leading nowhere.

Study of My Great, Great Grandfather Outside the Family Farm

The air is so much denser here,
the birds *swim* through it.
So many birds eating so many insects,

so many songs, and the rise of it pulling
at your voice so you sing a hymn into the hot July air.
Your blood is full of soil and crops and hares, your land

is quartered by barn owls and kestrels,
weasels and stoats, the early rise of a dog fox,
a badger sett in the far north corner.

They have yet to burn the orchard down,
they have yet to pull the hawthorn up.

The skylarks are rising, pulling at the blue
like lifting a curtain.

Boulder Song

The boulder sings like a tuning fork sings,
vibrating with the glacier's movement. Listen.

It is a sound forced through
the drilled holes of a mammoth tusk, through
the hollowed contours of ice.

The glacier's world is a long, slow thunder
of destruction.

The boulder is singing back. Listen.
It is a call played through a flute made
from the thigh bone of a cave bear.

The boulder rolls through the dream-time
to stop in a great lake formed from the glacier's body;
a miracle of solid-gas-liquid states.

The glacier is a god of fertility now,
a god of fish and reeds and water.

The lake shrinks away, the boulder
rises as a steeple in a drowned village.

Listen: a bypass is approaching, a bridge,
a train-track, a town; out of the shallows,
out of the farmland, out of the heavy machinery
of creation. Listen.

Self-Portrait Existing as a Fat Woman

A Duplex

I am immovable, a mountain.
But my body is a thing of backgrounds.

I am a green screen for your backgrounds.
You project onto me your Botticelli, your Stone Age goddess.

Some of my actions are those of a goddess.
I am able to increase or reduce my effect on gravity.

I swallow worlds whole, for ballast, for gravity.
It is only your attention that prevents me escaping.

My attempts to escape make some people rich.
I am a wide-mouthed bucket holding shame.

I am a wide-mouthed bucket holding your shame.
My body is unstable, the scree of myself moves.

I exist only in the way my body moves.
I am impossible to conquer. I am not your mountain to conquer.

Quern Stone, Sewerby, Grave 41

when they / pushed / their weight
against the quern stone / she
was still alive / she was still alive
when they / were standing on the stone
the stone with its memory
of the grinding work of women
when they / were pushing it
into her / lower back lower
into the fleshy parts
the secret parts of her /
on this fresh air morning,
this blackbird-singing morning,
the stone is lifted away
she / is opened up to the blue
of the sky and the sound
of the sea far below

Sometimes I Pretend I am a Dog

When we are alone together
I allow myself to become pack.

We stop and I sit
and you move about the place

in silence. Sometimes we both
lie down with our sides against

the parched earth and let our eyes close.
When people are near, I act

as if I am also a person. Mostly
it is just us and the Wolds or

the chalk farm roads and wind turbines
and rocks and cloud shadows,

the fast pace of the sun over great distances.
You do not look at the view as I do

but you understand how to move within it.
When I was a child, I hid under the teacher's desk

and would speak only in dog. I did not pretend
to be a dog. I *was* a dog. I willed myself to canine.

The family dog was my brother. I ate from his bowl,
slept in his bed. I long to be that animal again.

Sometimes I test myself to see how dog
I still am. I run my tongue along my canines

and feel for the movement of my ears.
I slouch my back, and pull my knees up

let my spine fall between my shoulder blades.
Sometimes I climb a fallen tree or a boulder

like that and it pleases me, and it pleases you
to see me down at your level. This is joy.

In these moments I feel as the earth must feel,
and I feel as the glacial till must feel and

what it might be to exist only in sensation.

Twelve Hour Working Day as a Golden Shovel

In a *Spectator* article, in 1995, Boris Johnson described working-class men as
"likely to be drunk, criminal, aimless, feckless and hopeless"

Long past teatime, stew warmed to a crisp, Dad comes home, likely
as not still smelling of the last bus he's cleaned down. He's too tired to
get changed, watches the news through closed lids. There will be
a time to recover, when we are all to be quiet. After he's drunk
the tea Mam pours him, he watches *Crime Watch*, the criminal
element, faces worn to bones by drugs or despair, recognises the aimless
wandering of folk with no jobs. We play Lego round his feet, the feckless
dog sits too close to the electric bars, burning the velvet of his ears and
Dad kneels, shifts him, knowing the dog'll just do it again, that it's hopeless.

The Internalisation of Imposter Syndrome by the Rural Working Class Writer

her face is a cocoon
her face is the paper of a wasps' nest
she peels it off and holds it out
where it flutters in the wind

  she lets it go

now her face is exposed skin of cool damp moss
the colour of deep silent thinking
the colour of still days with no noise
                        her other face has landed in a hedge
                    the hedge begins to see itself as   *liminal*

now she is driving with the window open
breathing in her own flat vowels
and her chest is filling with the sea at Filey

now her heart is a seal in the bay
now her heart beats for the first time
in two years   now she homes her body
into the glacial valley   now she is laid
in the valley and the slopes of its sides
are the perfect fit for her   now her heart
is a Shap granite boulder   rolled into her chest
twelve thousand years ago

My Dad on the Dark Side of the Moon

When I think of my dad at the end
I am thinking of the way we accompanied him
to the hospital   as if accompanying him
to a religious   ceremony
the way all   jewellery was removed
all hair how   he carried no mobile phone
how he slipped   into a place of being entirely alone
and how we   quietly recognised this
as something   people have done for thousands of years
and how it is   necessary when you are a warrior
or an astronaut   to go places and face fears on your own
I am thinking of him   carrying his *Bag for Life*
across the car park and   how we didn't hug
and how we barely said   goodbye and how
he passed from one moment   into the next
and how I imagined him drifting   into the dark side
of the moon and how we four left with   gravity
and density tapped the   landline
and   said

Ground control to Major Tom

because we are a family that jokes
through our trauma and how those jokes
didn't protect us from the pain

I am thinking of the way
the surgeon opened him like a letter

I'm thinking about the surgeon's soft hands
to which my father would have joked

Never done a hard day's work in his life

and how hard the work that the surgeon did was
how he tried to reel my dad back from the black emptiness

my dad's skin shimmering gold in the light
from an enormous sun as he spun and spun away from us

how the surgeon pulled on those frictionless space ropes

                                      how they could not get the traction
                                          needed to return him to us

Concealment of Birth, 1846

the prisoner is walking
        walking   in the field
on the cliffs   the prisoner is
 walking   walking
in the field   the prisoner
walked into the barn
into the field
        into the field
into the field
  under the hedge   the prisoner is on the ground
  under the bush

the prisoner is warm weather

the prisoner is broad leaves
the prisoner is grass   unclean
the prisoner is guilty
into the field
into the workhouse

(A found poem from *The Morning Post* 18th July 1846)

Excavating the Bone House

After Seamus Heaney

I

Up and over the tops leaving
the valley of the glacier below.

Up and snaking the car
on the crooked deer leg

of tarmac. Up
past the ploughed-out remains

of a long barrow. Up
and cutting straight through

a copse of oak,
up through the long-time-ago

of wood-cutters
and henge-builders.

The gear stick rolls
beneath my palm

like a bone in a socket,
vibrating my arm to its root.

Then sky. Then the wide flat Wolds
and up and out over the tops

to the loneliness of farmhouses
and tree-clustered howes.

Howe from the old Norse *haugr*
for hill, for mound, for burial place.

Howe Hill, Howe Field, Howe village
Willy Howe, Duggleby Howe

where the *Gypsy Race* raises
its magical winterbourne path.

Howe too, as a shallow dip
as a hollow place, a place to be filled

and *how*, as in *for what purpose*
still the question, *for what purpose*

and the emptiness of the word
and the filling of the word with myth

and the fairies in the mounds
and a dragon sleeping there

and a giant prising earth
and hurling it across

the Great Wold Valley
and me in my child-toy car

crossing this place of questions
and ancestry, up and away

to secret dips and deep paths
that sit below my sight line, below

the horizon where the sea pools
and moves.

II

In the ragbag of my mother-tongue
a Norse mōþir is passing me *Top*,
the name for high places, for places
from where folk can look down on you.

She, and her Old English sisters, pass me
bairn – a word so roundly woven, a baby
could sleep soundly in the vowel of it.

They are cleaning the *muck* from the boots
of their lords, they are minding the *bairns*
in the *beck, rarving* them out of the *watter*,
pulling 'em up when they're *greeting* and bawling
slapping their arses when they won't stay still.

They are calling them *gawmless*. My mother
is calling me gawmless in her mother-tongue
the other mothers are *ligging* the bairns down
on a blanket on the grass, shouting *'ey up*
to each other, *'ey up* to themselves.

III

Now I dig down
to find the tongue
of my mothers

and find instead
my grandfather counting
sheep

Yan, tan, tether,
mether, pip, lezar,
azar, catrah, borna

in a language he can't
remember learning, in the old bone-house
of his own family language where
women make rag rugs by the hearth
and corn dollies from the harvest.
He still speaks in thee, tha, and thou.

He is counting in dry-stone-wall
from the henge-curve of a sheep fold.
The words move in greasy huddles,
the wind blows over the tops and down
from the drover's road in sheets of spring snow.

IV

In the valley of the glacier
the tops are the edge
of your world. You cannot
see over them. If you want
to get to books
and libraries, to BSc and PhD
you have to climb over the edge.

In the Dale of my mother-tongue
the tops are the flat top of my own head
where my mind is separated from the sky.
The tops form the roof of my mouth
where my flat vowels sound themselves.

The tops are the height to which I can reach.
The tops are the grimy extractor fans
of fish and chip shops, the marble
bathrooms of houses where we clean
other people's mucky dogs, or
the floor to ceiling windows
of the factory canteen.

When I climb towards my own tops
I am climbing myself, climbing my own body,
climbing my frame as a mountaineer,
as a solo hiker. I wear my accent,
my patterned scarf of Norse, Celt, Old-English
mother-tongue on my head like a crown
and I cut out my path with a flint knife
and I climb, I am climbing.

V

You, with your Norman name
and neat chin, your lion-pale
hair and skin, are so far
from the valley. My love,
you are my transport.

I slip onto your back
and you carry me
to a place of theatre
and office jobs and
cocktails and restaurants
and dinner at teatime. Soon
I think this is my world.

Here is where the dark carr-land
meets the sun coming over the tops.

My love, you are my sun.
I am always in the howe,
I am always in the dip
asking to be filled with the answer
by what means, for what purpose,

for what purpose? Waiting
for a shaft of light to illuminate
the centre of this place of burials.

VI

when I find the blackbird
skeleton, its tail feathers
still attached, it is tucked up
like a Neolithic burial,
a small howe, surrounded
by the dry leaves of last autumn.

No flesh is left, just articulated bone
and two dunn feathers that tell me
it was female.

I touch the tip of my finger
to the henge of its eye socket,
place my nail just under the ribs
in the deep valley of its heart,
feel the ridged tops of its vertebrae.

I feel for its wings, how they're attached,
how they are able to stretch out, as arms
from the body, how they must have lifted
the whole small map of itself into the air.

Before I place it down I feel along the top
of its skull, in its naked state
so much closer to the air, the sky.

The Tea Towel Game

she is so good at removing things
we barely realise they are missing at all:
from the top of the sideboard the everyday objects –
to be disappeared on the magic tray
a fork   a spool of cotton   a button
a fossil   a conker   a nice piece of flint
a small orange stone   a cone   a crow feather
a pin badge   a thimble   the pieces of
my mum's life   a tea towel
pressed white   laid across the objects   a magic trick and us
turned away   turned back   the big reveal
my mum's quick slender fingers removing   one thing at a time
one item   always a small item
what is missing
what is missing
one item   always a small item
my mum   removing   one thing at a time
turned away   turned back   the big reveal
pressed white   laid across   a magic trick and us
my mum's life   a tea towel
a pin badge   a thimble   the pieces of
a small orange stone   a cone   a crow feather
a fossil   a conker   a nice piece of flint
a fork   a spool of cotton   a button
from the top of the sideboard the everyday objects –
we barely realise they are missing at all:
she is so good at removing things

the day I hit a blackbird

all the world stopped   singing
while it arced across the road
like a clock weight on the up
the curve   never completed

                        the thud
                        was so small
                        so definite

I prayed then
to some bird-headed-god

knelt in the confessional
of my car

                        in the silence

Jackdaws

a mourning necklace
on the collar bones
of a beech tree

Metal Detecting

lead loom weight,
1978 penny
with portcullis
worn to nothing,

am I digging for the precious metal
of myself, or for real treasure?

a smooth curl of bronze
that fits the curve of my thumb,
glass bottle-stopper,
sheep's tooth.

Blackbird Singing at Dusk

The ear is the interface the pale rim of it   the place for the song of the blackbird is curved so softly into my neck   a physical place of winding ivy dense green fern curve a funnel for the blackbird song from a blackbird taut with the keen stress of existence from a blackbird silhouetted against the sunset   fading place of the day feet curved on the red roof of the garage opposite the living room   eye alert to movement there where I lie on the brown sofa with a glass of wine light passing through amber liquid and the window open and the funnel open and the blackbird   black light reflecting pouring its song over the rooftop warning other males   to turn and curve away not to roost where it roosts and my own space in my own room   the only place where I warn not to interrupt this moment of book   where a blackbird might own blanket and wine   a red rooftop   a place on a branch in the low limbs of a beech tree and a freshly cleaned room   where no fox might come no cat no dog no badger and the blackbird song which stops me where it stops stops the world in its beauty makes me turn the pale curve of my ear to it turning itself outward the hidden hole lets me funnel the sound into the brain under the black neat feathers the bird's ear pulling it back and raising me up listening to the creak of leather   the creak of leaves

Drone

Down into the green
where cow parsley is a reed bed,
the dog a seal slicing
through stems thick and purple.

The plants have grown themselves
a sheath-hand around each stem,
holding themselves back,
or comforting themselves.

I float five feet above
the hot-rain-tarmac. I rise
like the ghost of precipitation
and turn my baby face up to the sky.

Look down on me, I have the head of a saint;
campions form my head dress, apple-blossom
picks out the green of my eyes. I am
an offering to the ancestors. Jackdaws flock
and shoal around my body space,
my cheeks silvered by a pewter sun.
I exist only as this moment of green light.

Ground Nesting Bees

you come upon a massacre of bees
and stop to watch them dying in the road
and pick one up and move it to a leaf
and squat to look inside the nesting hole
and still yourself and push your lungs to stop
and move your face in close and press your tongue
against your gums and watch bees searching for their young
and feel the morning frantic with their loss.

Know this: at some point in the early hours
a badger came, its body a brooding power
of necessity and need, it sought to feed
here in the too-dry soil. It tore through weeds
and seized upon the nest and gorged. It slid
the soil aside to eat the larvae and it lived. It lived.

Slow Summer Poem of the Morning

Tattered paper of the zesty rose,
           cried-out tissues of the summer morning collecting on
                                  the station house fence
                                        platform of

blackbirds and goldfinch,
cats on the tracks.

All things must pass.

This dream time of blush-chested kestrels and swifts
high over the sheep fields, feeding.

                This dream time of green-gold wheat, weeks before
                              the thrum and throb
                              of the combine harvester.

All things must pass

the rouge of cherries
ripening on the branch

all things must pass

                                      all things must pass
                                      the heads of roses,
                the fledged starlings on the telegraph wires.

Miracle of the Solstice

and of the paddleboarders
floating on the rippled sea

and of the snail in the wet dew
and of surprise in the sun's heat.

Miracle of the warmed carpet
in a shaft of sunlight

and of the house
with the sleeping husband

and of the burble of coffee
and of the hum of the fridge.

Miracle of the fat pigeons in the road
and of the sun rising golden

and ancient
and of the hush of the sea

and the seagulls in the surf
and of the man who stopped walking

to watch the rind
of gold rise over Filey Brigg

and of the little salmon boat
and the tanker far out

and of the sun's beam illuminating
the campsite on the hillside

as if the campsite was a Neolithic tomb
and the sleeping holidaymakers

precious offerings.

Thirteen ways of listening to a blackbird

I
On broken wings
for two minutes and nineteen seconds.

II
A leucistic blackbird
is unable to deposit
pigment correctly into its plumage.
It is always recognisable.
It can never blend in.
It sings like it doesn't care.

III
The chutt-chutt of a blackbird
sifting through last year's leaves
as if it had a dozen things to do at home
but can't find its house keys.

IV
Terrible beauty of the blackbird
singing at the hospital window.

V
In a slip of early morning light
a female, the colour of turned earth
appears as a black note on the stave
of a telephone line.

VI
In the cathedral of a beech copse
two blackbirds echo each other
their songs arcing away as ripples
in a tiny mirroring of time and place
within the universe.

VII
After the underground conveyer belts
and the dull beat of the factory
a blackbird singing its heart out
in the 4 a.m. sunlight.

VIII
For four years
my bones were hollow, my cavities
stuffed with blackbird feathers. All my sounds
were dulled and yet, in the nest of my heart;
the chipped flint alarm-call of a blackbird.

IX
Sound of dad's car
pulling into the drive, radio so loud
I can hear every word clearly.
Sudden silence.
House door opening.
Blackbird filling the quiet.

X
The sparrowhawk
forces the blackbird
to contract
like a sonic boom.

XI
Twelve thousand years ago
a blackbird was singing
while the lake people
set up their camp.

XII

The air was heavy with heat.
The wine was a cold fire.
We counted the repetitions
of the blackbird's song.

XIII

Saintly death of the blackbird;
wings spread, eyes tight shut,
one speck of blood on the yellow beak.
But even in the silence that comes
after the sudden stopping of motion
I am carrying its song in my head.

Miracle of the Peas

I planted them too late,
never quite getting
the raised beds set up
or the compost turned
in time. But still, I went ahead
thumbing them
into the warm earth.

Weeks later they rose
strong and deep green
and I gave them
the benefit of the doubt,
raised supports of twigs
and string around them.

Within a day they'd
stretched
tendrils fine as hair,
reaching and grasping

and I saw, in a montage,
my hands rested on the wooden frame
of the raised vegetable bed
in the same way I'd rested them
on the edge of the factory belt
on the edge of a microbiologist's bench
on the edge of the shop counter
on the edge of the kitchen sink
on the edge of my writing desk

and on the edges of all the places
where I'd touched down, thumbed
myself into the earth and hoped to root,
and I saw myself

as if through someone else's eyes
giving myself the benefit of the doubt.

Dales Engineering

We drop my brother off to join
a skein of men
        men in boiler suits,

     I watch the suits. I watch as he becomes a wave
     among the many other waves.

Settling to a slow pause of evening.
Territory of the blackbird now. The factory permanently closed
        to workers who migrated to other plants.

Twenty years of nine o'clock come and go.

And go and go the geese over the flat roof.

I live with the ghost of the factory,
the wobble of myself reflected in the windows.

        The roof bruised with buddleia,
the structure peeling its man-made skin away
to drop in thuds and rattles in the night.

Sunset is gone from the office windows,
     cleared like leaves
        off the trees in winter.

One day they knock it down.

Sara Lee

11.30 p.m., winter.
A road of deep indigo tarmac

and bare trees doused
in frozen mist. I pull the car over

near the campus to fill
my black sky with the white leaves.

It's cold and sharp and empty
as a dreamless sleep there

outside the college where I didn't go
the halls and lecture rooms that I don't know.

I used to work in a frozen food factory
where the steady beat

of underground conveyer belts
kept the time. There were no windows,

no trees. Line six, a new station every half an hour,
fingers numbed even inside double gloves.

Inside me is a room, a walk-in freezer
where accidental snow is still falling.

A Guide to Metal Detecting

Lay yourself down on the earth:
pelvis, leg, ribs
against the solid green of it.

Listen for the footsteps,
lost conversations.

One. Two. Three.
Then the pleasure of the flip,
the plug open, a portal:
the first look into the black
for the green of copper,
the untarnished rind of gold.

Leave yourself there
in the wet-grass-shadow,
the trail of yourself,
sometimes a dip in the green
where you sit and wait out the rain.

Oak   sycamore   hawthorn

blackthorn

blackbird   sparrowhawk.

Eleven

I want you to know
that we are happy.

I want you to know that we laugh.
That some days I think I have forgotten
what you look like.

That we sit on the patio
drinking wine and sometimes
we don't think of you at all.

That I can't imagine you
at the age you would be now.

I want you to know
that I keep your clothes
near our bed,
where I can see them.

That your photo is faded
and everyone in it looks dated,
except you.

I want you to know that sometimes
I live in the days of your death.
That sometimes I can smell
the bereavement suite, sometimes
the sound of the heart monitor wakes me
and the sound of the fan whirring
and the smell of toast on the ward
and the squeak of trolleys wheeling drugs
in the corridor and you in the Moses basket
is all there is.

I want you to know that on those days
it is difficult to let you go again.

I want you to know
that today isn't one of those days,

I want you to know that today
I carry you up to the cemetery like
a goldfinch on my shoulder
and that you bob away in the air
and then back again, and that
it makes me happy
to imagine us this way.

The Cat Brings Me a Live Sparrow, April 2020

It jerks and rises, then slips
behind the vase on the windowsill.

Now it is up to me to hunt,
to gently pull the balsa wood bones,
grip carefully the spindled ribs
beneath the slight grease
of dun feathers.

I hold its heart beneath my thumb.
The bright-black ring of skin around its eyes shines.

Before I even unfurl my hand
it's over the fence, over the road;
a dip and rise of familiar flight:
two metres, four metres   gone.

Body of the Shrew

Crushed by the car's wheel
last meal of berries
spread red in a small island
on the tarmac

a small island of shrew
and of exotic tunnels
of grass grown into archways
high as a house around him

and the deep alien scent of mud
as all things smell of mud
and of breathing and movement

as all things breathe and move.

Talking to My Father as We Drive to the Second Chemo Appointment

He is seventy. He is seventeen. He is
driving a Rington's tea van miles from home.

He is driving a United Buses coach
down Staxton hill, a pissed-up woman
screaming for her life as the snow blurs
the road to white and the bus loses its traction,
slews its shadow over the edge.

He is a tenant farmer's boy riding a red bike
home from school. The seat creaks, the bell
stiff with rust. He rides up Burn's Lane and finds
the orchard pulled up; hedges gone.

They have used old oil to fire the bonfire.
The hedge-sparrow nests ignite,
black smoke billows into the farmyard.
There is nowhere to settle here.

Woe Water Fails to Rise

Our bed was a raft above a chip shop
above a thatch of nesting kittiwakes
above the Gypsy Race; the Woe Water
pouring its heart out into the harbour below.

Our house was a juddering structure
of beach views and sky views
and up-close views of your face
and views of the carpet and views of the walls.

The Woe Waters licked my feet and seeped
through the blue carpet where your boots
were two Neolithic standing stones.

My Woe Waters have been sleeping
twenty-five years dry and still
Woe tries all her tricks to tempt
a rise, to tickle water from my chalk bones.

She pulls her voice back from the rhythm
of the shore, sucks the salt from it.

She's handing me her watery heart, she's handing me
her rise. But I am water too. I'm done with Woe.
I've poured myself into the shape of something new,
I've poured myself into a glass of something clean and true.

19th Century Cowbell

I dream a marbled cow the colour
of a Grimshaw moonscape knelt
to drink. The leather collar snapped,
the little bell knelled its last,

fell beneath
the clove of a hoof
and was folded neat
as a bun case

neat
as an offering bowl
into the mud of the bank.

I stop to watch
the fine kite of a kestrel hunting.

The regular train passes
its people along the hedge line.
They are a baton handed along and along, given this still
moment to look at.

A leveret is hidden so well
I swipe the metal detector over its head
like a blessing, my foot inches from its face,
its pain inches from happening.

When it runs, I touch my hand
to the heat left in the grass
by its tawny body.

The brass bell comes up from earth green
with a hundred years of its own silence.
I meet it head on with my own.

The water in my village

flows upwards, from the ground.

We float over it on brick
and pan-tiled rafts.

The stream rises brown
with the froth off the fields
and rushes beside the black road.

It rises in marshland
and seeps, seeps, seeps
into the bark of beech trees.

The wren darts through the hedge.
The long-tailed tits gather in a row,
above the cup and ring marks

appearing in the puddles. The old river
rises in the village with the sound
of flint and bone, copper and bronze.

Thoughts on Deer Grazing at the Cemetery on the Day My Daughter Would Have Been Twelve Years Old

Two deer coming down out of the woods
each foot a needle sewing

footprints to the dew.
Two roe adults the colour

of last year's leaves,
picking through the headstones

gentle as mist, eating the heads
off the flowers. It pleases me to think

I have been leaving offerings
at your altar, yellow roses

to the spirits of this place,
inviting them to be near you.

Intensive Care Unit Two

Each bay is a tether to a person dreaming.
I imagine them floating above, the wires and drains,
the chill beat of the ventilators snaking up
as a baby's cord snakes to its mother.

The soft light of the universe shines here,
and a singing of shushed alarms in this place
of deep dreams and decisions. One man, wild
and unshaven, is rowing a boat above his bed,

trying to reach the sanctuary of a harbour.
Down below, his body thrashes one arm,
the rowing intensifies. Another man is dreaming
of filing. Endless papers, endless reports

before he is allowed back home.
When we reach the bay of my father he is far away,
the cord of the machines a long taut line reaching up
into the starry clouds. We can hardly see him.

I imagine him in this dream place, journeying out
to the tussocked fields of his childhood, the family farm.
There are cows to bring in. *Come beast*, he says gently,
herding them back towards the byre. We touch his body

while he sleeps, try tempting him back with tales of his other life:
the fish that need feeding, the chickens that need sweeping out,
the apples in the orchard that are ready to be picked.
My mother, a wren at his ear, calling and calling.

Thirteen

This year you come to me in the rain,
your name a sudden shock
on the lips of a passing woman

to her daughter, out walking in the lane.
The two recede. Her daughter's back
is sullen under black layers.

The passing cloud
of your impermanence drifts through
and for a second I am in the dark

lush of your watery air. For a second
I think I feel you there, your shadow
bridging the gap between us,

petrichor of your shampoo, slight
weight of your body next to mine,
columns of you drifting across

the distant valley of me.

Boulder Returning in Echoes of Self

If I was the boulder, I was rock scraped
by ice for ten thousand years.

If I was the glacier, I was almost stopped
but never quite coming to rest.

If I was the valley, I was opened
with force and the whole of me
falling forward slowly.

But the valley was opened up
to the sky and I shifted my weight
with the force of its opening.

Though I looked like I was still,
I was fluid as slow water
beneath a frozen exterior.

Though I was scraped, I was granite:
uncrushable, time-rider, earth maker.

Acknowledgements and Thanks

With thanks to The Society of Authors for a foundation grant given to me in 2021, which allowed me a short period of financial stability in which I could work on this collection.

Versions of these poems have appeared in *The Friday Poem, Under the Radar, One Hand Clapping* and *14 Magazine*.